Lance Armstrong

Lance Armstrong

Michael Bradley

BENCHMARK BOOKS

MARSHALL CAVENDISH
NEW YORK

Benchmark Books
Marshall Cavendish
99 White Plains Road
Tarrytown, NY 10591-9001
www.marshallcavendish.com

Library of Congress Cataloging-in-Publication Data

Bradley, Michael, 1962–
Lance Armstrong / by Michael Bradley.
p. cm.—(Benchmark all-stars)
Includes bibliographical references and index.
Contents: Welcome to the club—Beating the odds—The big fight—Tour de Lance—Piling it on—Five and beyond—Player statistics.
ISBN 0-7614-1761-3
1. Armstrong, Lance—Juvenile literature. 2. Cyclists—United States—Biography—Juvenile literature. 3. Cancer--Patients—United States—Biography—Juvenile literature. [1. Armstrong, Lance. 2. Bicyclists. 3. Cancer—Patients.] I. Title II. Series: Bradley, Michael, 1962– . Benchmark all-stars.

GV1051.A76B73 2005
796.6'2'092--dc22

2003028007

Photo Research by Regina Flanagan

Cover: AP/Wide World Photos
AFP/Corbis: 2–3, 6, 12, 14, 16, 21, 32, 34, 40; AP/Wide World Photos: 18, 22, 23, 26, 28; Reuters New Media/Corbis: 8, 10, 11, 27, 29, 33, 41; Eric Gaillard/Reuters; Al Tielemans/Sports Illustrated: 20; DPPI/Icon Sports Media: 24, 30, 35; Photo News/DPPI/Icon Sports Media: 36; Tom Simon/DPPI/Icon Sports Media: 38; Reuters: 39; Damian Strohmeyer/Sports Illustrated: 42.

Series design by Becky Terhune

Printed in Italy

1 3 5 6 4 2

Contents

Tour de France winner Lance Armstrong cycles proudly with the flag of the United States of America.

CHAPTER ONE

Welcome to the Club

There was still one day to race, but Lance Armstrong knew. His rivals knew. The world knew. A fifth straight Tour de France championship was his. He had conquered the most important competition in all of cycling, a *grueling* twenty-one-day *endurance* test that can cause even the most talented racers to crumble. As he stepped to the podium to accept the yellow jersey, a symbol given to the race's overall leader after each stage of the Tour, Armstrong was on the verge of becoming just the fourth man to win the event five times.

"Welcome to the club," said Bernard Hinault, one of the other five-time champions.

Armstrong had clinched the win in typical fashion. His rivals had stayed in their hotel rooms on the morning of the next-to-last stage of the race, keeping clear of the wet roads and fighting the rainy weather. But Armstrong and Johan Bruyneel, the director of Armstrong's U.S. Postal Service team, had driven the 30-mile (49-kilometer) course. They were looking for dangerous spots, tough turns, and anything that could give Armstrong an edge. The extra work paid off. During the race, Armstrong's closest challenger, Jan Ullrich, had fallen on the wet road, dropping fourteen more seconds behind Armstrong. Ullrich's coach had videotaped the course that morning, while Armstrong was out inspecting it himself.

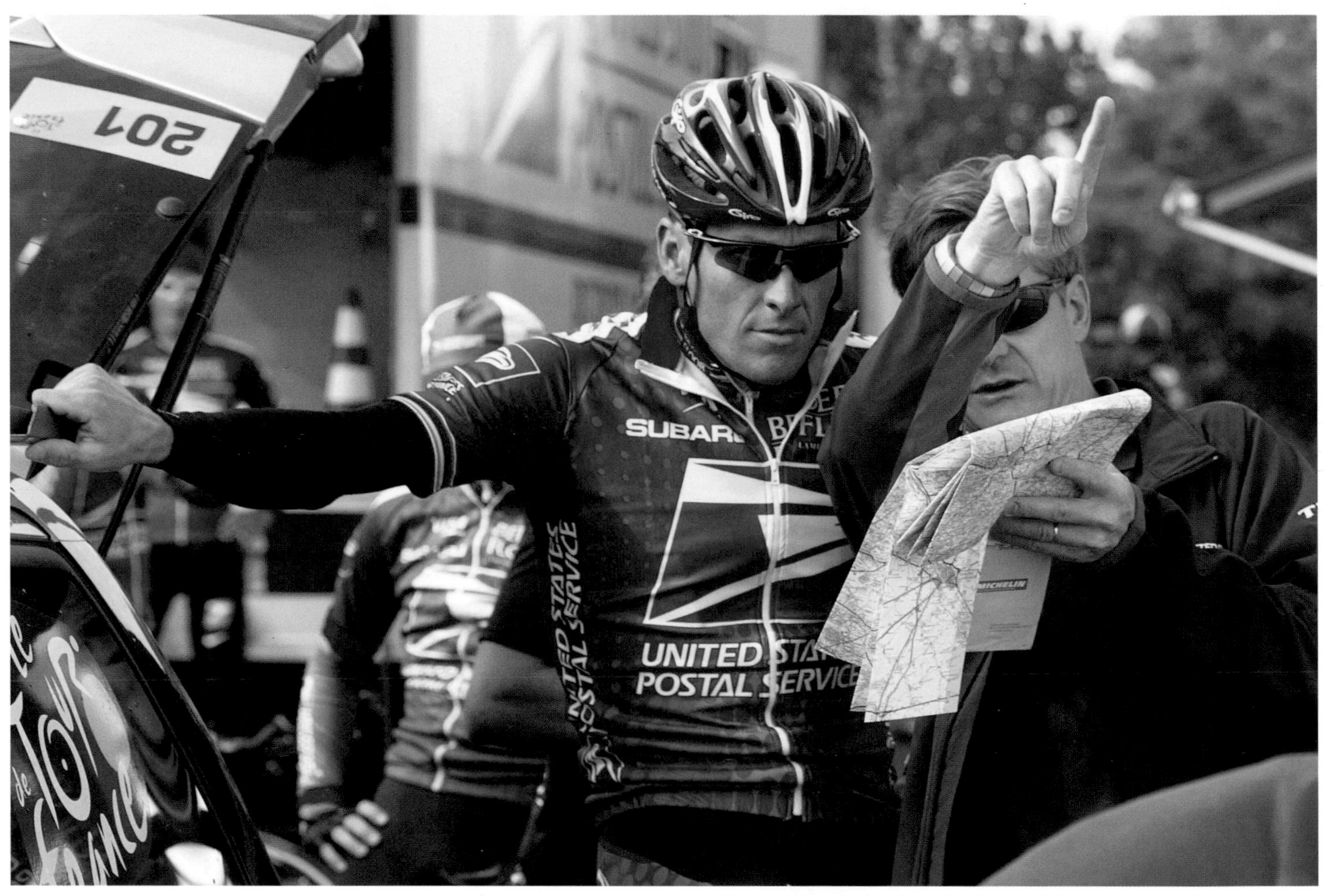

Armstrong checks his map before making a training run for the Tour de France.

It was yet another example of why Armstrong is the best. Nobody works harder. Nobody trains harder. Nobody wins more. "I am very passionate about cycling," said world-class Dutch rider Erik Dekker, "but I cannot match Lance. Mentally, he is unique." Armstrong's drive comes courtesy of victory over one of the toughest adversaries known to man. When he was just twenty-five, Armstrong was diagnosed with cancer and given less than a 40 percent chance of survival.

But he fought through surgery and exhausting treatments to do more than just survive. He is now one of the most popular athletes in the world and clearly the most successful cyclist. Armstrong receives three hundred letters a week from cancer patients. They are looking for hope and strength to help them in their fight. He tries to answer each one, sending a message of hope and some of his never-quit spirit. His Lance Armstrong Foundation has raised millions for cancer research. No wonder companies pay him $200,000 to hear his *inspirational* message, hoping their employees will be *motivated* to work harder. In a country where cycling is well behind sports such as football, baseball, and basketball in popularity, Armstrong has triggered a huge boost in interest. Each summer, Americans scan the sports pages to see how their rider is doing in France.

"I don't think cycling in the U.S. is going to become any more popular than it is now," said former U.S. Postal Service team director Frankie Andreu. "Lance has the perfect story. He gets cancer. He comes off his deathbed to win the Tour de France, and then he does it [again]. If that didn't make the sport explode, I don't know what will."

None of it has been easy. He was raised by a single mom in Texas and grew up to be a rough-edged Lone Star cowboy on two wheels. Success early in his career earned him money and trophies, but many in the cycling community were turned off by his *brash* attitude. Still, Armstrong rode on, only to run straight into a wall. He got cancer. This caused him to lose weight, and the treatments led to his losing his hair. But he didn't lose hope. And when the doctors gave him the all-clear sign, he went to work like never before. "Fear should never fully rule the heart, and I decided not to be afraid," he wrote in his autobiography, *It's Not About the Bike*.

He worked harder than anyone else. In May 2000, Armstrong was training in France's Pyrenees mountains, preparing for the Tour de France. He had just finished climbing seven and a half miles (12 km) up Hautacam, a dangerous mountain with a narrow, twisting road. It was 36 degrees Fahrenheit (2° Celsius) and raining. But something wasn't right. When

The Tour de France

To Americans, the Tour de France is an annual cycling tour through the fields, cities, and mountains of France. To Europeans, it is the Super Bowl, Kentucky Derby, and Indianapolis 500 rolled into a month-long celebration of sport.

The Tour began in 1903 and now covers from about 2,000 to 2,500 miles (3,300 to 4,000 km) during three weeks in July. It is divided into twenty or twenty-one "stages," each of which takes place during a day and can vary from sprints to long, painful climbs through French mountains. Nearly two hundred riders compete every year.

Riders try to win individual stages, but the real glory in the Tour de France comes from wearing the yellow jersey, or *maillot jaune* as it is known in French. The Tour's overall leader is awarded the shirt and gets to wear it during competition as long as he is in the lead.

The French get extremely excited about the Tour. More than 10 million people line the roads throughout the country to watch in person, while another 40 million keep track every day on television. When the final stage rolls to its end, down the storied Champs-Elysées in Paris, hundreds of thousands are on hand to cheer the winner.

Armstrong prepares for the eleventh stage of the Tour de France.

Armstrong made it back down, his coach was waiting with a towel and warm jacket. But Armstrong wasn't ready for that. Nope, he needed to make the climb again. Just to be sure. "I gotta suffer a little every day, or I'm not happy," he said. Later that summer, during the Tour, Armstrong took the lead with a breathtaking climb up Hautacam, leaving other riders in the dust. Afterward, his coach held a picture of Armstrong from that raw May day. "This is the secret of Armstrong," he said.

But not everybody buys it. Many in the cycling community, especially French journalists, accuse Armstrong of cheating. They say he takes drugs that make him stronger. They forget that he trains six hours a day. They seem unaware that he is so careful with his diet that he

Armstrong is the leader of the pack during a training run for the Tour de France.

Armstrong, who has recovered from cancer, is a source of inspiration to the sick. Here, he shakes hands with Angel Ludena, a boy with leukemia.

weighs his food before eating it to make sure he isn't getting too much or too little. They also don't seem to realize that he has seen what it's like to be near death and has decided that he will make every day a full-out ride to the finish. Armstrong has never failed a drug test, but that doesn't stop the critics. And they can't stop him. They never will. They can't. Too many sick people are depending on him.

"I know they're out there," Armstrong said of the cancer sufferers who look to him for inspiration. "Sitting there with those drip poles [delivering medicine into their veins], lying in those La-Z-Boys thinking, 'This guy had the same exact thing I do. If he can do it, I can do it.' I think of them all the time. I want to motivate them. They motivate me."

And what great things they accomplish together.

Yellow-jersey wearer Armstrong stands with his mother, Linda Mooneyham, onstage at the Tour de France.

CHAPTER TWO

Beating the Odds

Lance was born on September 18, 1971, in Dallas, Texas. His mother, Linda Mooneyham, married twice while she was still a teenager. Her first marriage was to Lance's father, Edward Gunderson. Her second was to Terry Armstrong, who adopted Lance, but whom Lance did not like. According to Lance, Terry Armstrong beat him with a paddle. The marriage was short-lived, and Lance spent most of his childhood living alone with his mother.

That was a good thing for Lance. Linda was a rock-solid constant for her son, even though she had to work hard to pay the bills. The two lived in Plano, a small town just north of Dallas. There, Lance developed his love of competition and his ability to overcome great odds. All he had to do was watch his mother. She began working at a fast-food restaurant but eventually worked her way through other jobs and finally earned a position selling real estate. When she told Lance to "make a negative a positive," she was speaking from experience.

"She *instilled* all her drive, motivation, and toughness in me," Lance said.

And so Lance went about his life with a burning desire to succeed, no matter what the odds. "I've always been better when I've had things stacked against me," he said. Linda was

Lance Armstrong is once more ready to go!

right there next to Lance as he fought to get over the *hurdles*. Since she was only seventeen when Lance was born, she was more like an older sister. But she took her responsibilities as a mother quite seriously. She fed him, clothed him, and made sure he had a home. And when Lance started playing sports, she was there every step of the way.

At first, Lance tried team sports—football, basketball, and baseball. It didn't work out too well. He didn't run fast and wasn't all that skilled in throwing, shooting, or hitting. Anything that involved endurance was his game. He could run forever. So, Lance became a long-distance runner. When he started running *competitively* in fifth grade, Linda drove him to races every weekend. Then came the swimming. Linda would drive Lance to practice and treat him to a twenty-five dollar Jet Ski ride afterward. Before long, teenage Lance was on a bicycle, riding 80 miles (128 km) to the Oklahoma border and back. Linda sat by the phone, waiting for his calls from gas stations along the way. Most of the time, Lance would make it all the way home. Other times, he would ask Linda to come pick him up because he was too tired to continue.

By the time he was in eighth grade, Lance had combined the three sports and was competing in *triathlons* across Texas and the nation. He enjoyed working by himself and mastering the sports. He even kept a daily journal of his training. In high school, Lance won two national age-group triathlon championships. He was tough and driven to win like few of his competitors. "I was a kid with about four chips on his shoulder," he wrote in his autobiography. Four chips were enough, but three sports were too many. Lance decided to concentrate on the one he enjoyed the most.

"One problem with the triathlon was that I didn't like the swimming all that much," he said. "It seemed everyone went into the water at the same time, thrashed around and pretty much came out of the water at the same time. Then, on the bike, everyone was drafting, staying close together. So, the race basically became a [6.2-mile, or 10,000-meter] run, which was my worst part. I looked at what I did best, what I liked best—riding the bicycle. I went with that."

Lance's full-time cycling career began at age sixteen. It was not long before he was beating men in their twenties. He logged hundreds of miles a week, training like few others. He didn't care about the pain, or the loneliness. Linda was always waiting for him at the end of the ride, and her strength carried him up and down roads throughout Texas. Lance was still in high school when he was earning $20,000 a year in cycling prize money. He was paying for his car and food but still living with Linda. He needed her. Once, when he was fifteen, Lance went to Chicago alone to compete in a triathlon. When he arrived at the hotel where he had made reservations, he was told there were no rooms. So, he called Linda. Linda called the manager and worked things out. Years later, she recalled the event. Once he was settled down, her son called back. "Mom," he said, "you won't believe it. I have a room on the top floor. There's a phone in the bathroom."

Lance made it through high school, graduating at age eighteen. It was time to go on. So, he moved alone to Austin, which sits about 150 miles (240 km) south of Plano, Texas. It was time to start his new life.

And start pedaling.

At age twenty-five, Armstrong was diagnosed with cancer. It kept him out of the cycling for a while, but when he came back, he was even stronger.

CHAPTER THREE

The Big Fight

On October 2, 1996, Armstrong heard perhaps the most frightening sentence anyone can hear. "You have cancer."

That awful *diagnosis* seemed impossible. Here he was, a world champion cyclist, one of the rising stars on the world bike riding scene, with cancer. And not just any cancer. This was a particularly deadly brand that had begun in his *testicles* and had spread. To his lungs. To his brain. His chances of survival were just 40 percent.

"I thought the same thing everybody thinks when he hears the word cancer," Armstrong said. "I thought, 'Oh, my God, I am going to die.'"

The trouble had started at the end of September, a few days after his twenty-fifth birthday. Armstrong began coughing up blood. His right testicle swelled to the size of a baseball. This was not the usual physical price (aches, pains, sprains, pulled muscles) he paid for training so intensely. This was worse. Far worse.

And it couldn't have come at a worse time. For the past three years, Armstrong had been one of the top young cyclists in the world. In 1991 he was the U.S. Amateur national champion. The following year, he turned professional, joining Motorola's team, and in 1993 he captured the

> **"I thought the same thing everybody thinks when he hears the word cancer. I thought, 'Oh, my God, I am going to die.'"**
> **—Lance Armstrong**

World Championships. He had ridden in the 1992 Olympics at age twenty and finished fourteenth in the road race. He won the Tour DuPont, America's top multistage race, in 1995 and 1996. He even won a stage in the 1992 Tour de France, becoming the youngest rider ever to do so. Nike had signed him to an *endorsement* contract, and the French cycling team Cofidis had inked him to a $2.5-million deal.

Along the way, Armstrong won many fans and made more than a few enemies. Americans loved his hard-charging style. He wasn't about to let anybody pass him, even if it was a more established teammate. That was a huge violation of cycling tradition. The sport is careful to protect its stars, and lesser teammates are expected to help the main riders succeed. In 1991 Armstrong was riding for the American national team in an eleven-day stage race in Italy when the coach asked him to hold back to let a more established cyclist win. No way. Armstrong won the race, even though the angry Italian fans—who wanted to see the sport's heritage upheld, even if it was an American winning—littered the road with tacks in front of him as he rode to victory. Armstrong may have been successful as a racer, but he had a lot to learn about cycling.

Robert Mionske, Lance Armstrong (front), and Marty Jemison in action on the tour.

"He thought he was *invincible*," Armstrong's cycling friend John Korioth said.

How a Cycling Team Works Together

When Lance Armstrong crossed the finish line after the final stage of the last five Tour de France races, he was celebrated as the champion, an honor he has richly deserved. But he will be the first to admit that he had help. A lot of help.

"Americans don't understand that cycling is a team sport," Armstrong said. "They see a guy on a bike. They think: 'individual sport.' At times, it is. But I could never, ever win the Tour de France without the team. Never."

Teams have nine members. There is one top-flight rider, whom the team is trying to propel to victory. The others take turns as *domestiques*, the French word for "domestic servants." Outside of the cycling world, domestics are people who work in homes, performing daily tasks. For cycling teams, domestics handle the hard, thankless work, such as delivering food and water to teammates during a race.

Everybody else has a specific job in each stage of the race. Perhaps one U.S. Postal Service team member will be asked to ride out quickly, setting a fast pace that will tire competitors out, while Armstrong hangs back to make a late run. Others will be asked to ride just ahead of Armstrong, cutting through the wind and allowing him to *draft* them, so he does not need to work as hard at pedaling.

During longer stages, different team members take turns in the lead. They'll ride in front a few miles and then drop back. That allows Armstrong to save the heavy work for later, when he needs to be at his best.

Being a team member sounds like a thankless job, and it can be. But not on the U.S. Postal Service team. Armstrong is extremely grateful to his teammates, and splits up his Tour de France winnings (about $350,000) among team members. In 1999 he gave each rider a bonus. Armstrong makes more than $1 million a year in prize money and endorsement deals, so he can surrender his Tour prize to his teammates.

Tour de France yellow jersey Armstrong rides among his U.S. Postal Service teammates.

Armstrong celebrates his victory in the men's professional road race in Oslo, Norway.

As it turned out, Armstrong wasn't that strong. At least he wasn't strong enough to keep cancer from invading his body. But after experiencing the inevitable period of gloom and despair, Armstrong decided to fight back. He knew it was going to be one tough battle.

"Cancer is smart," he said at the time of his diagnosis. "It's *aggressive*. It has *tactics* it can change and ways it can resist. When I raced, I said, 'Whatever it takes to win.' Well, this whole thing is just that: Whatever it takes."

On October 3, doctors removed Armstrong's right testicle. But that was just the beginning. Armstrong worked with doctors at the Indiana University Medical Center to devise a plan of treatment that would whip the cancer and still allow him to ride. He decided on surgery for the brain *tumors*, because a course of *radiation*—the customary treatment—could result in a slight loss of balance. That was one of the worst things for a cyclist.

When it came time for *chemotherapy*, a collection of medicines administered to kill cancer cells, Armstrong again didn't choose the more familiar treatment because it could result in somewhat diminished lung strength. He chose a drug, ifosfamide, which had awful short-term side effects, like nausea, vomiting, and dizzyness, but wouldn't harm his lungs. Over the next three months, Armstrong underwent surgery and then three courses of chemotherapy. He lost his hair, a typical side effect of chemotherapy. Armstrong was in great physical condition, so he had very little fat to lose. Instead, he lost muscle—about 15 pounds (7 kg) of it.

But Armstrong never lost hope. He took 30-mile (48-km) bike rides during the periods between his chemotherapy treatments. He survived the treatments and then waited for good news. On October 2, 1997—exactly one year after hearing the awful news that he had cancer—Armstrong got the information that he had fought so hard to hear. He was cured. This wasn't remission, in which the cancer could come back. He was told he was cured. No more cancer. And no more worrying about the future. While he had been fighting cancer, he met and married Kristin Richard. She became pregnant with their first child, Luke, who was born in 2000. Lance is father to two other children, twin girls Isabella Rose and Grace Elizabeth, who were born in November 2001. Life had been good before. Now, every day was a gift.

Armstrong is perched on his bike in downtown Austin, Texas, before a charity ride to benefit the Lance Armstrong Foundation, a nonprofit volunteer organization formed to aid cancer research.

"Before cancer I was always worrying about what I was going to be doing five or six years down the road," he said. "That's [bad]. It's a terrible way to live. When I was the sickest, I just decided, 'I'm never going to waste another day thinking about tomorrow. This is it. Today is all I have.'"

Armstrong returned to cycling stronger than ever. The weight loss gave him a leaner, lighter body, one perfect for climbing. He changed his training to build more and more endurance. Armstrong began to get better. He was ready to take aim at the biggest prize in cycling.

The Tour de France.

Lance Armstrong rounds a corner during the 1999 Tour de France.

CHAPTER FOUR

Tour de Lance

It was a dramatic moment, to be sure. On a French mountain, surrounded by some of the world's greatest cyclists, Armstrong made his move. Moved away from his competitors. Away from those who wondered whether he could be a major figure in the sport.

Away from cancer.

During the ninth stage of the 1999 Tour de France, a nasty climb that usually separates champions from pretenders, Armstrong won the title. Even though there were eight stages remaining, his bolt to the front of the pack put him in charge. He would win his first Tour de France.

The first eight stages of the race had been back-and-forth affairs. Armstrong had captured the yellow jersey (given to the Tour's overall leader) after the first stage, on July 4. "I really wanted to take the yellow jersey. . . . That's cool," he said. But Armstrong surrendered it again in the second stage, to Jan Kirsipuu of Estonia. No problem. He took it back again after the eighth stage and sat in first place as the Tour moved into the mountains. That would be the test. In all of his Tour experience, Armstrong had never fared well during the backbreaking climbs. He may have been the leader, but the race's favorites—Ivan Gotti,

Armstrong is flanked by his wife, Kristin (l), and his mother, Linda, after he wins the 1999 Tour.

Fernando Escartin, and Alex Zulle—were expected to take over from there. Expected to. Did not.

In the ninth stage, with Gotti and Escartin next to him and Zulle close by, Armstrong burst away, startling his rivals. He pulled away and kept climbing. Faster. Stronger. He built the lead steadily over the next stages, conquering twenty-five mountains in the process. When he finally crossed the finish line in Paris, twelve days after his dramatic breakaway, Armstrong had completed a miracle comeback. He had won by more than seven minutes over second-place Zulle and was more than ten ahead of third-place Escartin.

"I'm in shock," Armstrong said. "I'm in shock. I'm in shock. I would just like to say one thing: If you get a second chance in life for something, go all the way."

Armstrong had gone all the way—and then some. Not only was he probably the planet's most famous cancer survivor, he had proved to the cycling world that it was wrong to underestimate him. It was a message to Cofidis, the French team that had signed him to a professional contract but dropped him after the cancer diagnosis. It was a call to all those suffering from cancer that it could be done. They could win.

> **"I'm in shock. I'm in shock. I'm in shock. I would just like to say one thing: If you get a second chance in life for something, go all the way."**
> **—Lance Armstrong**

Armstrong raises his arms in victory after he wins the first mountain stage of the 1999 Tour de France.

The victory was dramatic and historic. But it had a price. Armstrong's bolt to the front was so fast that it created doubt in the minds of many members of the cycling community. Jean-Michel Rouet, a French cycling writer, watched the move on television and was immediately *skeptical*. "That climb was so amazing," he said. "It was so quick."

Others felt the same. There was just no way someone could bolt away from the world's best climbers without some help. Illegal help. From the moment Armstrong took the lead in the French mountains, the *speculation* began. By the time he had won, it had turned into a chorus of doubt. "There is no evidence against him, so he is innocent," Rouet said at the time. "But he is a strange case. He is on another planet."

Much of the dispute focused on a drug Armstrong had taken during his cancer treatment. Erythropoietin, or EPO, helps the body create more red blood cells, which are crucial during chemotherapy, when the drugs used to kill cancer cells also attack some healthy cells. When athletes take EPO, they can train harder and longer, without any extra pain or fatigue.

For that reason, EPO was banned by the international cycling body, which considered it a means of cheating. It had become a threat to the cycling community. During the 1998 Tour de France, an entire French team was disqualified when its trainer was found with 234 doses of the drug.

Armstrong keeps his balance no matter how sharp the corner!

Armstrong had taken it during cancer treatments, but he had stopped once he returned to cycling. Riders are required to provide samples of their urine on demand at times throughout the year to test for the presence of drugs. All of Armstrong's drug tests were clear of banned drugs or other substances.

"I can only assert my innocence," he said. "I have never tested positive. I've never been caught with anything."

In the long run, Armstrong would be cleared of any wrongdoing, but the whole affair

A spectator dressed as an angel looks on as Armstrong climbs the Galibier Pass of Switzerland.

had strained his relationship with the French people and media. Some would never believe he was not using EPO. Others thought he was a typical American, rude and nasty, and now a cheater. Armstrong tried to make friends with the French. He even learned their language. In the end, he decided to let his cycling speak for itself.

"I came back from the illness, and everybody said, 'You're not gonna do anything, you're not gonna win anything, you're not gonna finish anything,'" Armstrong said. "So I said, '[Forget] you. Why don't I just focus on the biggest, baddest race there is?' So I did."

In the coming years, the world would find out just how strong that focus was.

Once again, Armstrong is the leader of the pack!

CHAPTER FIVE

Piling It On

The wind was howling. The rain was pouring down. Sideways. It was cold. It was dark.

It was Lance Armstrong time.

On July 10, 2000, the Tour de France headed up the Pyrenees, fighting the steep incline, each other, and the elements. It was a miserable day—for most of the 162 riders. For Armstrong, life was beautiful.

"To me, it was like a sunny day at the beach," he said. "An absolutely perfect day."

That's what happens when you have survived cancer's hardest punch. Even the worst weather cannot bring you down. And even though Armstrong had begun the tenth stage of the world's most famous bicycle race in tenth place overall, practically six minutes behind leader Alberto Elli of Italy, he was happy. Happy to be alive. Happy to be back in the mountains, where no one could stay with him.

Just as he had the year before, when he charged wildly away from the pack, Armstrong made his move. By the time this stage was over, Armstrong was in first place in the overall standings, 4:14 ahead of second place Jan Ullrich of Germany. Armstrong's will had again prevailed. "When I saw Armstrong, I had the impression I was watching someone

The front-runner in the 2000 Tour de France rides along Leman Lake.

descending a hill I was trying to scale," said French racer Stephane Heulot. Heulot was not the only cyclist in awe of Armstrong's talent. "No one can fight him," German cyclist Walter Godefroot said.

Indeed, Armstrong was invincible during the 2000 Tour de France. He won his second championship by a comfortable margin, further tightening his grip on the cycling world.

As a result of his amazing victory, more whispers and outright accusations surfaced. Again, critics said he was using banned substances to improve his stamina and strength, even though Armstrong continued to pass every drug test administered. In explanation of his winning streak, Armstrong revealed more of his training regimen. Part of his success was because of a complete reshaping of his body. Armstrong no longer had heavy muscles throughout his neck and shoulders. He was leaner (down to 160 pounds, or 73 kg, from a high of about 180 pounds, or 82 kg) and built more for the demands of a multistage race like the Tour de France. And he was logging more hours, every single day, than any of his main competitors. And loving it.

"What is sacrifice?" he asked. "You suffer a little during a training ride. You suffer during a race, and I like that. I would be really upset if I never had the opportunity to suffer. I would go crazy."

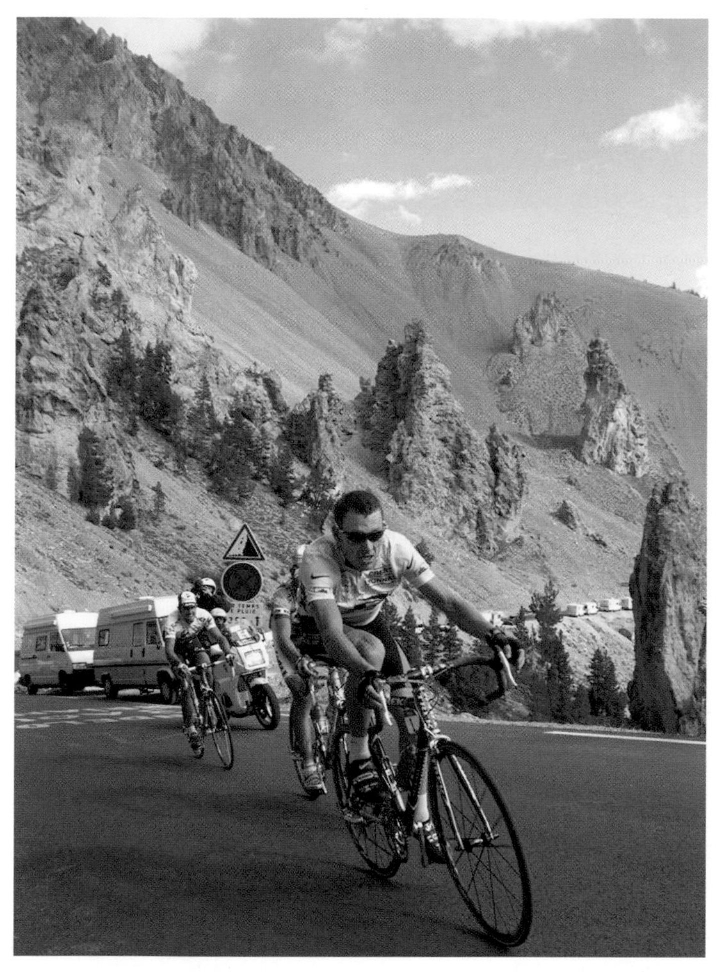

Armstrong climbs the Izoard mountain pass during the fourteenth stage of the Tour.

In the 2001 Tour, Armstrong made the others suffer, particularly his rival, Jan Ullrich. Again, it was in the mountains that the great American had made his move. During the thirteenth stage, a 138-mile (222-km) haul that included trips over six different mountain peaks, Armstrong took over. He had begun the day in third place, nine minutes behind François Simon of France. And though Armstrong fell behind France's Laurent Jalabert for a long stretch, he eventually made up the ground and took the lead. By day's end, he had the yellow jersey, and, for all intents and purposes, his third Tour de France championship.

"It's been a long time since cycling had a real boss," said Johan Bruyneel, director of Armstrong's U.S. Postal Service team. "Right now in the Tour de France, people consider Lance the boss."

The win brought Armstrong a step closer to the sport's greats. And they began to recognize that. Belgian Eddy "the Cannibal" Merckx, a five-time Tour winner, believed that Armstrong had great things ahead of him, even though he had already accomplished so much. "Armstrong could win five [Tour de France titles], he could win six, he could win seven," Merckx said. "As long as he stays focused on the Tour de France."

Armstrong was focused, all right. But it would not be easy. In 2002 he would need considerable help from his teammates to win his fourth Tour de France title. The trouble started in the ninth stage during a time trial. A time trial is an odd race, in which cyclists ride alone, against only the clock. After all have finished, their times are calculated, and a winner is determined. In this particular time trial, which is usually an Armstrong specialty—he had ridden three of the Tour's ten fastest time trials ever—he finished eleven seconds behind Colombian Santiago Botero. "I can't lie and say I'm not disappointed," he said afterward. "In the past, sometimes I'd think, 'Man, I'm really going fast.' Today, I didn't have that feeling."

The good news was that the mountains lay ahead. That is where Armstrong had traditionally taken over. And that's how it went in 2002, with a

Great Cyclists

If Lance Armstrong wins a sixth Tour de France in 2004, he will be considered by some to be the greatest cyclist of all time. But it will be easy to make an argument for several others. Here are a few of the best.

Eddy "the Cannibal" Merckx. This flying Belgian is a living legend in his country for winning the Tour de France five times, from 1969 through 1972 and again in 1974. He rode with a passion and a ruthless power that overwhelmed his competition. Many consider him the greatest ever.

Bernard "the Badger" Hinault. A Frenchman, Hinault did not dominate the Tour over a period of consecutive years. Instead, he showed his greatness during an eight-year stretch (1978 through 1985), during which he won the Tour in 1978, 1979, 1981, 1982, and 1985.

Miguel "Big Mig" Indurain. This powerful Spaniard was a dominant force on the cycling scene throughout the 1990s, winning in France from 1991 through 1995. He was simply more powerful and stronger than his competition and was able to grind them down over the course of the lo

Three past Tour de France giants (l to r): Belgium's Eddie Merckx, France's Bernard Hinault, and Spain's Miguel Indurain link hands as they attend a gathering of cycling enthusiasts.

"What is sacrifice? You suffer a little during a training ride. You suffer during a race, and I like that. I would be really upset if I never had the opportunity to suffer. I would go crazy."
—Lance Armstrong

twist. Instead of breaking away by himself, he let his teammates do the early work. The U.S. Postal Service riders took turns in front of the lead pack, setting a quick pace, but allowing Armstrong to draft them. As other riders fell away, the U.S. Postal team forged ahead. Finally, near the top, Armstrong was set for his move. He churned on, riding away from his challengers and into the overall lead. "Basically, it's like following a jackhammer," challenger Joseba Beloki of Spain said after the stage. "That's what finally got to me, the constant up-down beat. It was clear there was no way I was going to follow that speed."

Lance Armstrong flanked by Joseba Beloki of Spain and Raimondas Rumsas of Germany during the final stage of the 2002 Tour de France.

Armstrong won the 2002 Tour by 7:17 seconds over Beloki, putting himself one win away from inclusion with some of the sport's greats.

Was there any doubt he would get it?

And he's off the seat! Some of those hills require an extra push on the pedals!

CHAPTER SIX

Five and Beyond

It was a crisis, pure and simple. The 2003 Tour de France had moved into the mountains, and it was winning time for Armstrong. He always won in the mountains. That's the way it had gone in his four previous Tour victories. Armstrong stayed close during the early stages and then broke everybody's spirit with an amazing climb up an impossibly steep mountain. And he wouldn't even breathe hard while he did it.

Not this time. When Armstrong arrived at the finish line of the first stage of riding in the Pyrenees, he was losing time. His overall lead was a mere fifteen seconds over longtime rival Jan Ullrich, and it was fading. The great Lance Armstrong was *vulnerable*, and a whole collection of riders was poised to pounce on the fading lion.

"It's obvious I'm not riding as well as in years past, and I don't know why," he said. "Something's not clicking."

Armstrong wasn't worried about just the mountain stages. The entire Tour to that point had been a difficult pull. During one 29-mile (47-km) time trial, he became so dehydrated that he almost did not finish. The temperature had climbed to 104° Fahrenheit (40° C), and Armstrong, who had been suffering from a virus he had caught from his son, Luke, was almost completely dried out. "I had an incredible crisis," he said. "At one point, I felt like I was pedaling backward."

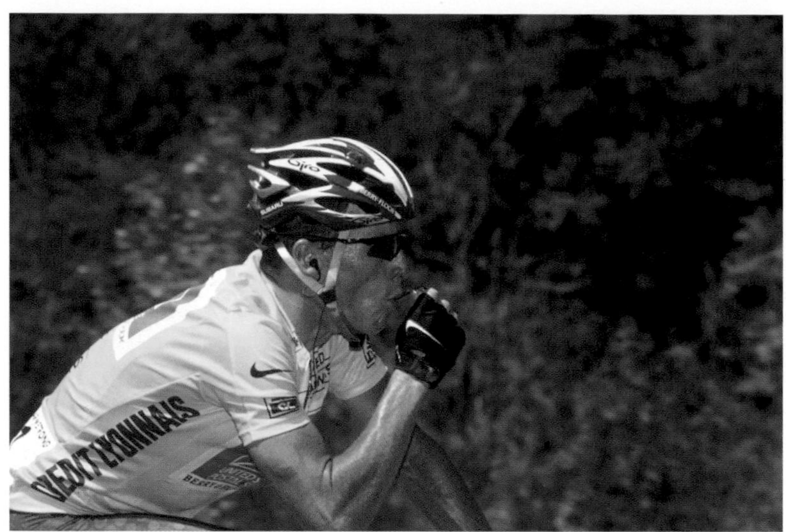

Lance Armstrong cycles through the woods in the 2003 Tour.

A couple of days later, Armstrong had another close call. On a less-steep climb in the Alps, rival Joseba Beloki, the 2002 runner-up, lost control of his bike and crashed. Armstrong was riding with him and had to swerve off the road and down a small slope of grass. He hopped off his bike and leapt across a small ditch to safety. Had there been a wall, a cliff, or any kind of hazard, Armstrong might have sustained a serious injury. Instead, he was able to resume riding. "That may have been the luckiest day I ever had," he said.

And so, the man who was bidding to join cycling's greatest names as a five-time Tour champion was struggling. If he hadn't succeeded, Armstrong would still be remembered as a giant. He was already the most recognizable cyclist in American history, a status which had earned him millions in prize money and endorsement payouts. By the 2003 Tour, Armstrong had lent his name to Coca-Cola, Nike, Subaru, and Bristol-Myers Squibb, a company that manufactures some of the drugs that helped him beat cancer. Armstrong had also been active in charities, devoting considerable energy to bringing hope to cancer sufferers. He had also worked with celebrities, such as U2 lead singer Bono, to help fight AIDS around the world.

Armstrong was determined, but fate had more misfortune in store for him. It would turn out to be just what he needed. Three days after the near-miss, Armstrong caught his handlebars on a plastic bag waved by a fan. (Spectators line the Tour de France course, often coming within a few feet of the riders.) Armstrong pitched forward and crash-landed

Armstrong crashed during the fifteenth stage of the 2003 Tour de France after his handlebars caught on a plastic bag carried by a spectator. Spanish rider Iban Mayo also fell, while Jan Ullrich of Germany swerved to miss the accident.

on the asphalt. Would this be a final, *insurmountable* barrier? No way. "After the fall, I had a big, big rush of adrenaline," Armstrong said. He told himself, Lance, if you want to win the Tour de France, do it today.

So he did. Armstrong embarked on one of his classic attacks and extended his overall lead over Ullrich to sixty-seven seconds. He would not give it up. Armstrong rode into Paris as the fourth five-time Tour de France champion. It certainly wasn't an easy ride, but if there was any cyclist in the world who could overcome the problems that had arisen, it was Armstrong. And when it was all over, the speculation started. Could he win six? Could he establish himself as perhaps the greatest cyclist ever?

"It's hard to imagine who can stop him, unless he has an accident. I see absolutely no reason why he can't win a sixth Tour, and I imagine him carrying on for many years to come."

—Eddy Merckx

"It's hard to imagine who can stop him, unless he has an accident," said five-time winner Eddy Merckx. "I see absolutely no reason why he can't win a sixth Tour, and I imagine him carrying on for many years to come."

And he's coming down the mountain here he comes—the Galibier mountain, that is, during the sixth stage of the 2003 Tour.

There was no reason to believe Armstrong could not do it again. Nobody has his toughness or desire. Nobody trains as hard. Nobody wants it as much. He has been to the edge and faced death, only to return stronger and more grateful for every day.

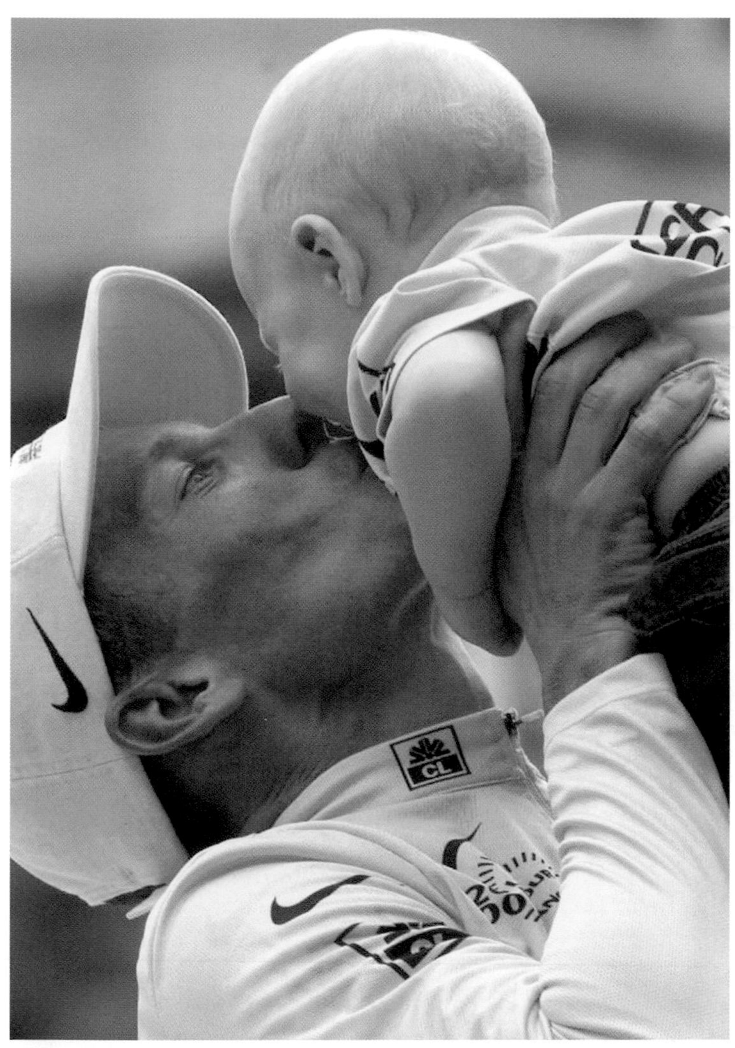

Armstrong celebrates his latest victory by kissing his son, Luke, who is dressed in a yellow victory jersey just like his dad's.

As tough as the 2003 Tour had been, the aftermath was tougher. He and Kristin decided to divorce a month after the fifth win. But if Armstrong is good at anything, it is overcoming adversity.

"I'm coming back, but I'm not coming back to lose," he said. "I'm coming back to return to a level I had in the first four wins, because this year's level was unacceptable. I don't plan on being this vulnerable next year."

He has fought for everything in his life, and if he says he wants to win a sixth Tour, we had all better believe him.

If Lance Armstrong says he is going to do something, it gets done. Again and again.

MOTOROLA
MOTOROLA
MOTOROLA
MOTOROLA
MOTOROLA

Stats Lance Armstrong

Team	**United States Postal Service**
Born:	**September 18, 1971**
Birthplace:	**Dallas, Texas**
Height:	**5'10" (178 cm)**
Weight:	**170 pounds (77 kg)**
High School:	**Plano (Texas) High School**

Career Highlights

1989: Qualified for Junior World Championships in Moscow, Russia.

1991: Won U.S. Amateur championship.

1992: Finished fourteenth in road race at 1992 Summer Olympics in Barcelona, Spain. Turned professional after the Olympics.

1993: Won ten titles, including USPRO Championships in Philadelphia. Won Thrift Drug Triple Crown. Won World Championship in Oslo, Norway.

1994: Won TDS Classic.

1995: Won Tour DuPont. Won Stage 18 of Tour de France. Named *Velo News's* North American Male Cyclist of the Year. Finished year ranked first in the world.

1996: Became first person to win back-to-back Tour DuPont titles. Won Fléche-Wallone, Belgium. Signed two-year, $2.5-million contract with French team Cofidis.

1998: Won Sprint 56K Criterium in first official race after recovery from cancer. Won Tour de Luxembourg, Rheinland-Pfalz-Rundfarht in Germany, and Cascade Classic in Oregon. Finished fourth in the Tour of Holland and fourth in the Vuelta a España (Tour of Spain). Finished season with a fourth-place finish in the World Championships in Holland.

1999: Won first Tour de France. Won Circuit de la Sarthe Time Trial. Finished second at Amstel Gold in Holland.

2000: Won second Tour de France. Finished second in Paris–Camembert race. Placed third in the French Dauphiné Liberé and Classique des Alpes races.

2001: Won third Tour de France. Finished second in Amstel Gold.

2002: Won fourth Tour de France. Finished second in Criterium International.

2003: Won fifth Tour de France.

Sources: http://www.lancearmstrong.com and http://www.uspsprocycling.com

GLOSSARY

aggressive—Rapidly spreading.

brash—Bold; not caring what others think.

chemotherapy—The use of high doses of extremely strong chemicals to kill cancer cells in the body. While killing the cancer, chemotherapy treatments also attack healthy parts of the body, causing weight loss, hair loss, and extreme weakness.

competitively—Testing one's self against the skills or talents of another or many others.

diagnosis—The process of deciding, through testing and analyzing, the nature of a certain disease or illness.

draft—To follow closely behind a bike rider who cuts through the wind for you, lessening any resistance you might face.

endorsement— Payment from a company in exchange for lending one's name to a product or service.

endurance—The ability to last or continue for long periods of time.

grueling—Extremely long and difficult.

hurdles—Barriers or obstacles that are difficult to overcome.

inspirational—Capable of inspiring others.

instilled—To put into someone or something, bit by bit. Teachers and coaches often instill confidence in their pupils over long periods of time by putting them into positions to succeed.

insurmountable—Something that cannot be overcome. In sports, this usually refers to a lead that a person or a team has built.

invincible—Unable to be defeated.

motivated—Extremely willing to perform a certain task or job.

radiation—The use of tiny nuclear particles to help clear the body of any cancer cells that might be threatening its health.

skeptical—Not willing to believe someone or something.

speculation—To think about the various parts of a situation and then try to predict what might happen.

tactics—The strategies used in a specific competition or job. These can be determined ahead of time or arrived at in the moment.

testicles—The two male sex glands that are contained in the scrotum, just below the penis.

triathlons—Competitions that require athletes to swim, run, and bike, one after another.

tumor—An abnormal growth in a part of the body that can be either harmless or deadly. Cancerous tumors must either be removed by surgery or shrunk by medicine or radiation.

vulnerable—Something or someone that can be easily wounded or injured.

Find Out More

Books

Armstrong, Lance, with Sally Jenkins. *Every Second Counts*. New York: Broadway Books, 2003.

———. *It's Not About the Bike: My Journey Back to Life*. New York: Berkley Publishing Group, 2001.

Christopher, Matt, text by Glenn Stout. *On the Bike with . . . Lance Armstrong*. New York: Little, Brown & Co., 2003.

Garcia, Kimberly. *Lance Armstrong* (Real-Life Reader Biography). Hockessin, DE: Mitchell Lane Publishers, 2002.

Web Sites

Lance Armstrong Online
http://www.lancearmstrong.com

United States Postal Service Pro Cycling Team Profile of Lance Armstrong
http://www.uspsprocycling.com/teamfile/04profile_armstrong.htm

INDEX

Page numbers in **boldface** are illustrations.